WORLD GEO...

TIME & CLIMATE ZONES

LATITUDE, LONGITUDE, TROPICS, MERIDIAN AND MORE

GEOGRAPHY FOR KIDS
5TH GRADE SOCIAL STUDIES

MW01153349

BABY PROFESSOR
EDUCATION KIDS

Speedy Publishing LLC

40 E. Main St. #1156

Newark, DE 19711

www.speedypublishing.com

Copyright 2017

All Rights reserved. No part of this book may be reproduced or used in any way or form or by any means whether electronic or mechanical, this means that you cannot record or photocopy any material ideas or tips that are provided in this book.

In this book, we're going to talk about time and climate zones of the world. So, let's get right to it!

The lines of latitude and longitude on a map help us with many things. They are used to pinpoint an exact location on the entire surface of the Earth. They are also used to separate time zones from each other. You can get a sense of the general climate of an area based on its location using the imaginary lines of latitude and longitude. They are like a giant imaginary grid on the Earth.

WHY ARE THERE TIME ZONES?

The Earth turns and makes a complete rotation in 24 hours. This is why an Earth day consists of 24 hours of time. Other planets spin too, but their days or the time it takes for them to make a complete rotation, are not the same amount of time as Earth's days are.

When we visualize the Earth turning, we imagine that it is turning on a pole called an axis, but, of course, there isn't a pole really there. It's just an imaginary device to help us understand how the Earth rotates.

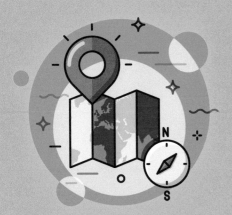

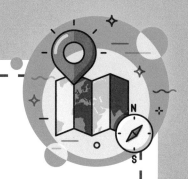

It might be morning where you are located right now, but on the opposite side of the Earth, it's the middle of the night. As the Earth turns, different locations are either receiving sunlight during the day or not receiving any sunlight at night.

If there were only one time zone for all of Earth, noon would represent different things to different locations. It might be midday for some locations, but it might be morning, evening or nighttime for others.

The Earth's Rotation

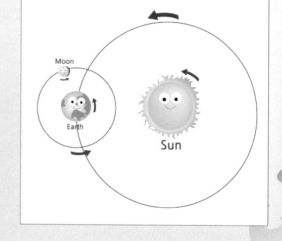

N

24hours

Night

Day

S

Earth

Sun

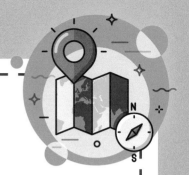

Toward the end of the 1800s when transportation was starting to get a lot faster, scientists got together to figure out a way to have different zones of time around the world. They researched the way the Earth moved on its axis to come up with a system that could be used everywhere.

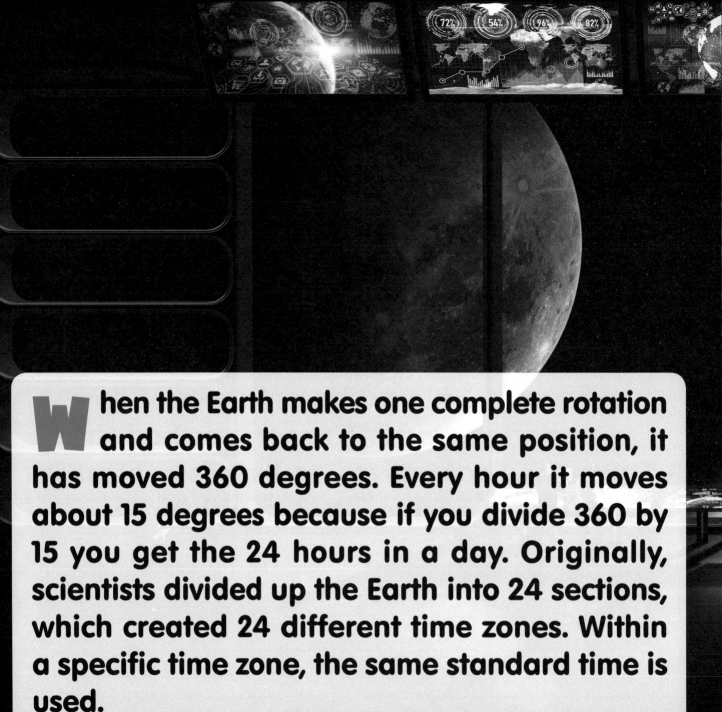

When the Earth makes one complete rotation and comes back to the same position, it has moved 360 degrees. Every hour it moves about 15 degrees because if you divide 360 by 15 you get the 24 hours in a day. Originally, scientists divided up the Earth into 24 sections, which created 24 different time zones. Within a specific time zone, the same standard time is used.

ASTRONAUTS STUDYING THE PLANET EARTH

WHAT IS LONGITUDE?

Imagine that you have a globe. The North Pole is at the top of the globe and the South Pole is at the bottom. If you start at the top at the North Pole and then draw a line to the South Pole you would have a longitude line, which is also called a meridian. The line is curved and bulges out at the equator.

These imaginary lines would need to be drawn 1 degree apart from each other, so there would be 360 longitude lines to travel the 360 degrees around the sphere.

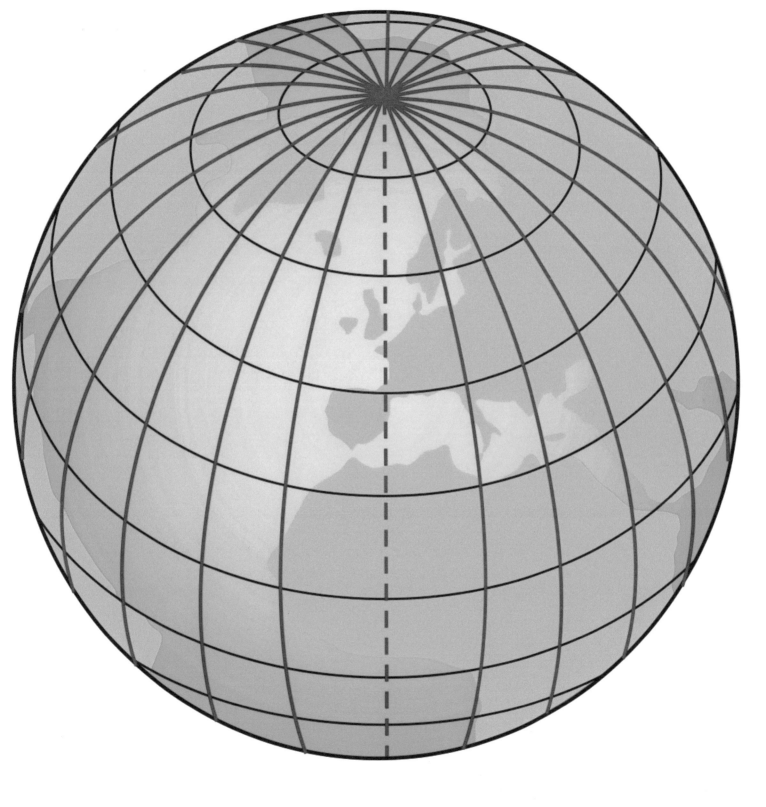

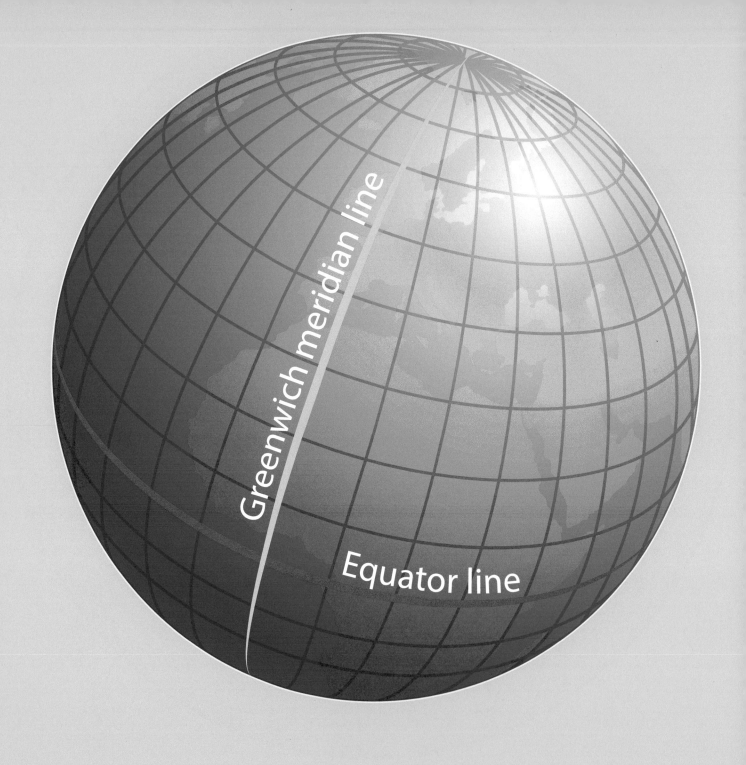

At the equator, since it is going from east to west, the longitude lines would make a right angle with the equator. There would be 15 degrees or 15 longitude lines for every time zone. You'll notice that the lines are closer to each other at the north pole or south pole and they are the maximum distance apart at the equator, about 69 miles apart. When you divide the length of the equator 24,874 miles by 360 this is approximately what you get--69 miles. The meridians converge to a common point both at the North Pole and at the South Pole.

The equator separates the world into a Northern Hemisphere to the north and a Southern Hemisphere to the south. However, to separate the world to describe it as an Eastern Hemisphere and a Western Hemisphere, the scientists had to pick a location. They picked the royal observatory for astronomers at Greenwich, England.

ROYAL OBSERVATORY, GREENWICH PARK, LONDON ENGLAND

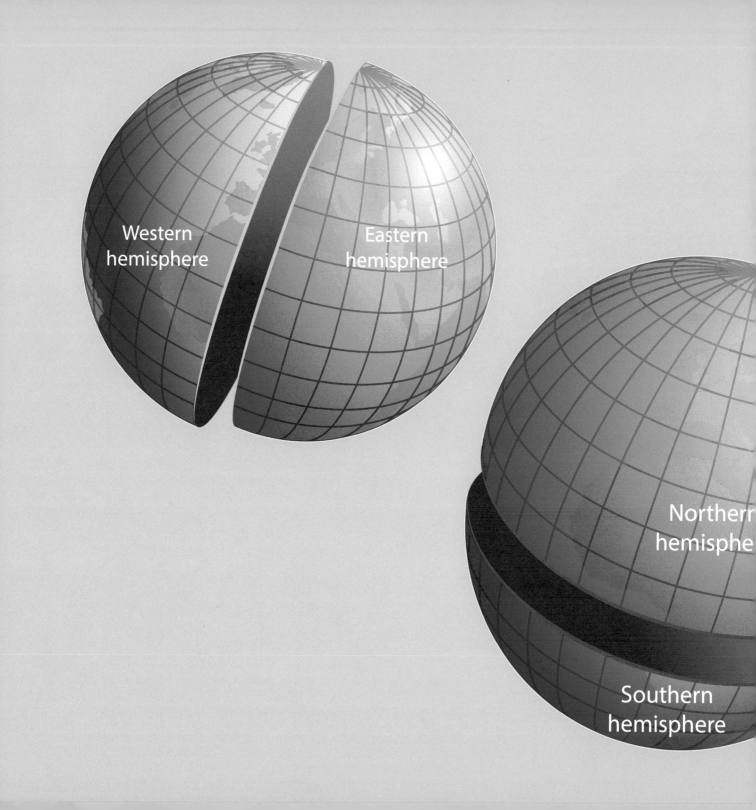

The meridian or line of longitude that goes through Greenwich is called the Prime Meridian and is the longitude of 0 degrees. Everything that lies in a position that is east of the Prime Meridian until you reach the meridian located on the opposite side of the Earth is the Eastern Hemisphere. Everything that lies west of the Prime Meridian until you reach the meridian located on the opposite side of the Earth is the Western Hemisphere.

Of course, there are locations in between different degrees of longitude as well. One degree is equivalent to 60 minutes and one minute is equivalent to 60 seconds so you can use these to give more precise measurements.

TIME ZONES AND LONGITUDE

The time at the Prime Meridian at Greenwich is described as Greenwich Mean Time or GMT. When you travel west toward the United States every section measuring 15 degrees represents a time zone, which is an hour earlier than the time in Greenwich. Every time zone east of Greenwich is one hour later than the time in Greenwich.

This means that it doesn't make any difference where you are; if it is noontime the sun is the highest in the sky and midnight divides the night in half from sunset to sunrise.

For example, if you reside in New York City, New York, during standard time your time zone is GMT – 5, which is five time zones in a western direction from Greenwich.

New-York

Lon

So this means that if it's 8 pm in New York on December 1, when it's standard time in New York, then it would be 1 am in Greenwich, the following day, because you are 5 time zones or 5 hours earlier. Daylight Savings Time changes these time periods.

In the United States, there are four time zones: Eastern, Central, Mountain, and Pacific. During Standard Time, if it's 4 pm on the West Coast it would be 5 pm in the Mountain time zone, 6 pm in the Central time zone, and 7 pm in the Eastern time zone.

Longitude determines time zones, but both longitude and latitude are needed to determine locations.

TIME ZONES WORLD MAP

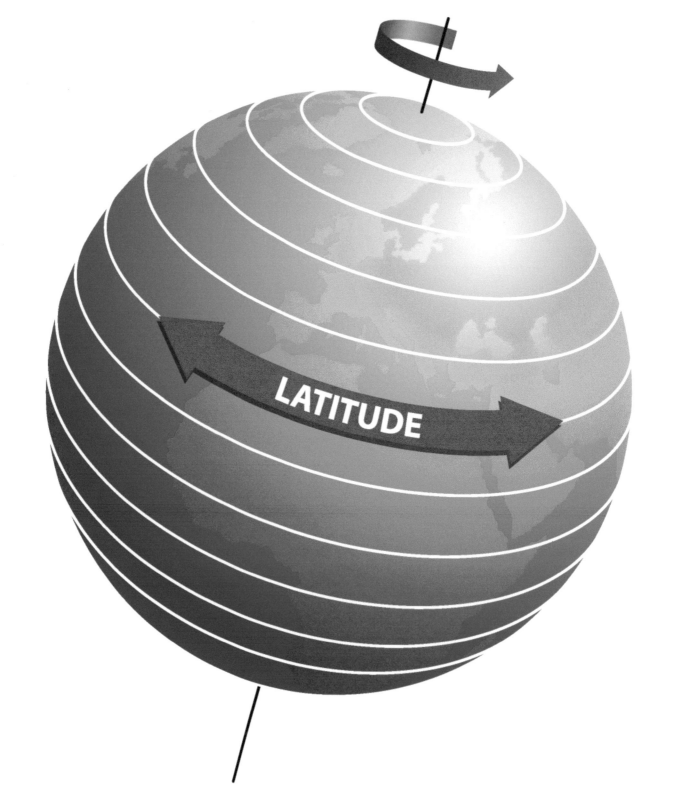

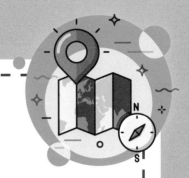

WHAT IS LATITUDE?

Just as longitude lines provide the east-west position of a location, latitude lines provide a location's north-south position. Lines of latitude are like hoops around the Earth from east to west. Unlike lines of longitude, they don't converge at any points but are always the same distance from each other.

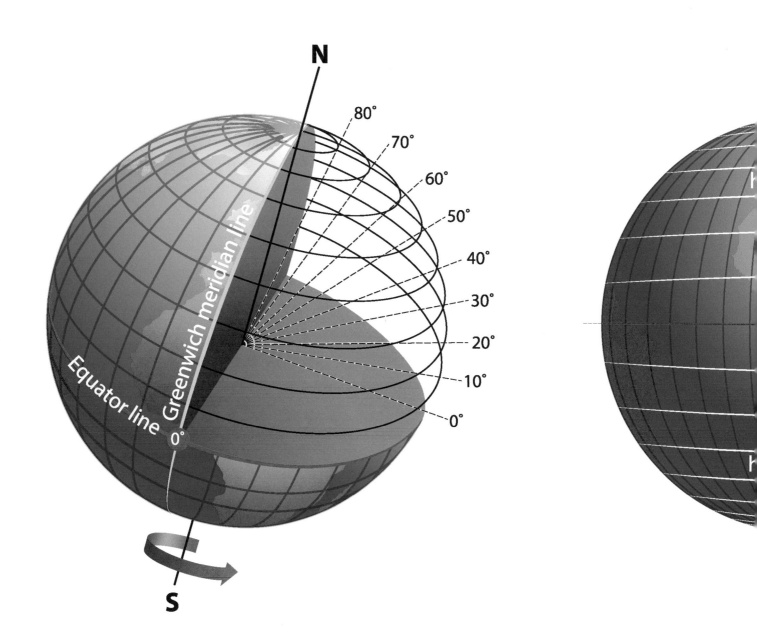

N

80°
70°
60°
50°
40°
30°
20°
10°
0°

Greenwich meridian line

Equator line

0°

S

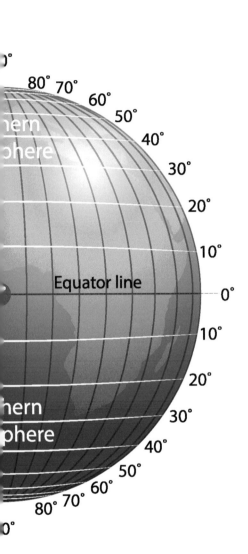

80° 70°
60°
50°
40°
30°
20°
10°
Equator line
0°
10°
20°
30°
40°
50°
60° 70°
80°

hey are about 69 miles from each other. The equator is at 0 degrees. Latitude lines above the equator are designated with north and lines below the equator are designated with south. On a flat map, latitude lines are horizontal while longitude lines are vertical. There are 180 lines or degrees of latitude.

Here are some important latitudes from north to south.

- The Arctic Circle, 66.5 degrees north
- The Tropic of Cancer, 23.5 degrees north
- The Equator, 0 degrees of latitude
- The Tropic of Capricorn, 23.5 degrees south
- The Antarctic Circle, 66.5 degrees south

S

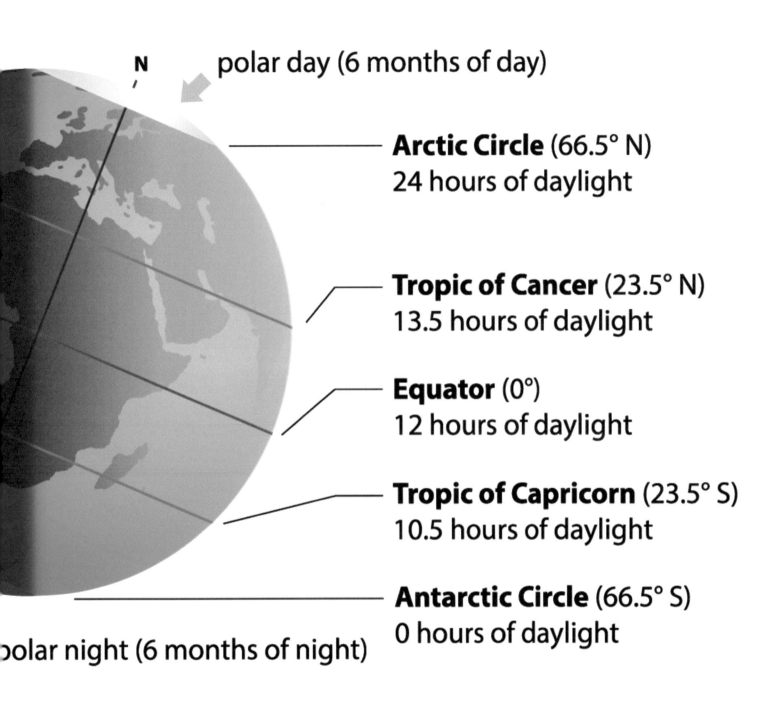

polar day (6 months of day)

N

Arctic Circle (66.5° N)
24 hours of daylight

Tropic of Cancer (23.5° N)
13.5 hours of daylight

Equator (0°)
12 hours of daylight

Tropic of Capricorn (23.5° S)
10.5 hours of daylight

Antarctic Circle (66.5° S)
0 hours of daylight

polar night (6 months of night)

WHAT ARE THE TROPICS?

The equator represents the part of the Earth where the temperature is the hottest. The landmasses in the world that lie between the Tropic of Cancer and the Tropic of Capricorn are described as the Tropics. These areas have sultry heat, heavy rainfall, and dense rainforests.

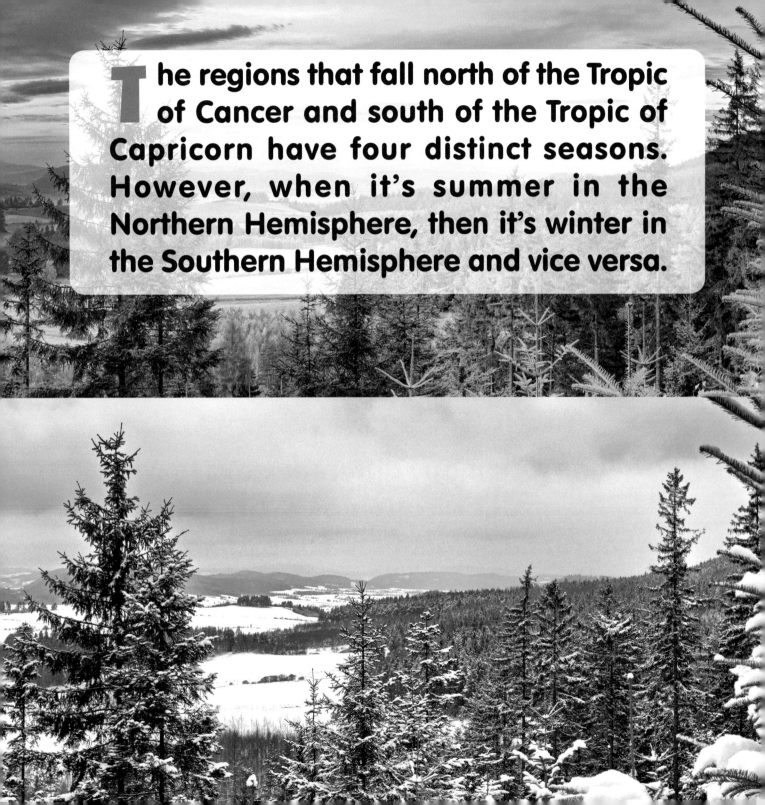

The regions that fall north of the Tropic of Cancer and south of the Tropic of Capricorn have four distinct seasons. However, when it's summer in the Northern Hemisphere, then it's winter in the Southern Hemisphere and vice versa.

LATITUDE AND LONGITUDE OF A LOCATION

There are many different ways to write the exact location of a city or other geographical location. For example, the location of New York City can be written the following ways.

- **Geographic Coordinates of New York City, New York**

  Latitude: 40 degrees 42 minutes 51 seconds North (of the Equator)
  Longitude: 74 degrees 00 minutes 21 seconds West (of the Prime Meridian)

- With symbols, this is written as:

  Latitude: 40° 42' 51"
  Longitude: 74° 00' 21"

- **Coordinates in decimal degrees for New York City, New York**

  Latitude: 40.7142700°
  Longitude: -74.0059700°

- **Coordinates of New York in degrees and decimal minutes**

  Latitude: 40° 42.8562'
  Longitude: 74° 0.3582'

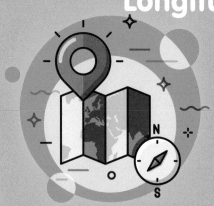

WORLD CLOCK

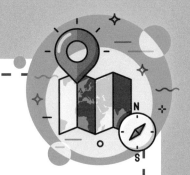

GMT VERSUS UTC

In 1972, the GMT was replaced by a more accurate way of measuring time, UTC, which stands for Universal Coordinated Time. Atomic clocks made it possible to measure the rotation of the Earth with more accuracy. For example, on December 31, a second of time is added or subtracted from the world's clock to synchronize GMT and UTC.

Even geological events can alter the rotation of the Earth. When Japan had a 9.0 magnitude earthquake, it shifted mass away from the equator and the Earth's day was shortened by 1.8 microseconds, which is one millionth of a second.

SUMMARY

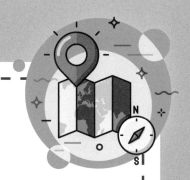

The lines of longitude and latitude are like an invisible grid on the Earth. The longitude lines establish the distance from the prime meridian at Greenwich, dividing the Earth into 24 different time zones. By using latitude and longitude, you can pinpoint a location anywhere on the Earth's surface. If a location on Earth lies between the Tropic of Cancer in the north and the Tropic of Capricorn in the south, then it has a tropical climate. Landmasses north of these two special latitudes have four seasons of the year, although if the Northern Hemisphere is experiencing summer, the Southern Hemisphere is experiencing winter.

Awesome! Now that you've read about the world's time and climate zones, you may want to read more about world geography in the Baby Professor book *Five Major Islands of the World – Geography Books for Kids 5-7 | Children's Geography Books.*

Visit

BABY PROFESSOR
EDUCATION KIDS

www.BabyProfessorBooks.com

to download Free Baby Professor eBooks
and view our catalog of new and exciting
Children's Books